A is for Asia

by CYNTHIA CHIN-LEE

illustrated by YUMI HEO

Orchard Books
New York

Cynthia Chin-Lee thanks Andy and Vanessa Pan, Allison and John Banisadr, William and Nancy Chin-Lee, Susan and Mohamad Banisadr, SuAnn and Kevin Kiser, Debbie Duncan, Cherry Lyon, Rita Seymour, Mary Elizabeth Wildberger, Nancy Farmer, Peggy Rathmann, Betsy Franco, Harold Underdown, Melanie Kroupa, Nancy Nordhoff and Cottages at Hedgebrook, Katy Obringer and the Palo Alto Children's Library, Marina Krakovsky, Jenny Lee, Norzin Lhamo and Sonam Lama, Jeff Iswandhi, Ravi Shankar, T. T. Nhu, Lin H. Chan and Pui-Laing Chan, Ever Bierke, Peter K. Marsh, Bonnie Kaslan, Kumar Gollabinnie, Zahid Khan.

Orchard Books

95 Madison Avenue
New York, NY 10016

Manufactured in the United States of America
Printed by Barton Press, Inc.   Bound by Horowitz/Rae
Book design by Chris Hammill Paul

10 9 8 7 6 5 4 3 2 1

The text of this book is set in 22 point Koch Antiqua.
The illustrations are pencil, oil, and collage.

Library of Congress Cataloging-in-Publication Data

Chin-Lee, Cynthia.
    A is for Asia / by Cynthia Chin-Lee ; illustrated by Yumi Heo.
        p.   cm.
    Summary: An alphabetical introduction to the diverse peoples, lands, and cultures of the world's largest continent.
    ISBN 0-531-30011-0. — ISBN 0-531-33011-7 (lib. bdg.)
    1. Asia—Juvenile literature. [1. Asia.] I. Heo, Yumi, ill. II. Title.
DS5.C56 1997
950—dc20
96-36346

Gamelan

Batik

ká

新年

折紙

熊猫

القُرْآن الكَريم

饭

САНИ

LOKUM

雨 傘

마을

Kalabaw

象棋

ГЭР

禪

To my father, William Chin-Lee,
my teacher and friend,
to the children of Asia,
and in memory of John and Mary Pan
*   —C.C.*

To my niece, Hojung   —Y.H.

A Note on Asian Languages

The languages of Asia are as varied as the cultures and countries that share this part of the world. On this spread you will find the words chosen to represent each letter of the alphabet, written in the appropriate Asian language.

Some Asian languages (like Tibetan, Hindi, and Arabic) have their own alphabets. Others (like Indonesian, Tagalog, and Turkish) use the Roman, or Latin, alphabet, the same one used to write English. Still others (like Chinese) don't use an alphabet at all, but instead use picture words called ideographs. The Japanese language uses a combination of picture words and its own two alphabets.

A is for Asia, one-third of the earth. Asia has the highest mountains in the world, the Himalayas, and the lowest basin, the Dead Sea. It includes not only China, Japan, Korea, and India, but also a large part of the former Soviet Union, most of the Middle East, and many of the island nations of the Pacific. Asia is home to more than half of the people in the world and birthplace to some of the world's oldest cultures.

ཨེ་ཤི་ཡ་

Asia in Tibetan

B is for batik, an Indonesian craft. Batik designers create a picture in wax on a piece of cloth. They then dye the cloth in different colors. Each time they dye the cloth, they remove the wax and apply it in different places, creating rich patterns, like these gold and orange ripples on a sea of blue.

Batik

Indonesian

C is for camels with one hump or two. Every year in Saudi Arabia, older boys race their camels in the traditional King's Cup Camel Race. Over two thousand camels and their riders bounce and jounce over the desert sand. The winner takes home a truck, prize money, and a gold dagger.

camel in Arabic

D is for dragon boats sweeping the water. On the river Yu in China and other places in East Asia, dragon boats decorated in the colors of the five elements—red for fire, yellow for earth, azure for wood, white for metal, and black for water—race to the finish. Drums drumming, banners waving, people cheer their favorite team.

龙船
dragon boats in Chinese

E is for elephants, graceful and imposing. Highly respected in India, elephants are still ridden in traditional wedding processions. The groom leads the way, riding a richly decorated elephant to the home of his bride, where he is greeted with garlands of flowers.

ड़ाथी

elephant in Hindi

F is for fish, a symbol of luck and long life. The fish is also a popular animal in stories and in games. In Vietnam, children play a game called Bite the Carp's Tail. The players form a single line. The first person, the "head," tries to grab, or "bite," the last person, the "tail."

cá

fish in Vietnamese

G is for gamelan, clanging and thrumming. An orchestra in Malaysia and Indonesia, the gamelan plays gongs, drums, bamboo flutes, and xylophones. Dancers leap and spin to the rich rhythms of the gamelan.

Gamelan

Indonesian

de, stone of heaven. Many people in East
e because they believe it will keep them from
iful and hard stone, jade comes in a rainbow of
ellow, lavender, pink, white, and green. If
d and kind, people may call that individual a

ကျောက်စိမ်း
jade in Burmese

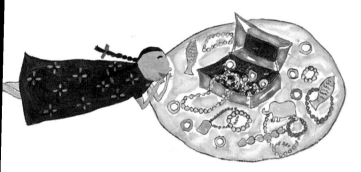

ites, fluttering in the wind. Dragon
butterflies dance in the skies where everyone
Kite-flying is a national pastime in Korea,
lar in other Asian countries. In Malaysia,
ighting contests where the object of the
opponent's kite down to the ground.

연
kites in
Korean

H is for Holi, a holiday of chills and thrills. A Hindu festival in India, Holi celebrates the colors of spring. During this holiday, children (and grown-ups) sneak up on their friends and drench them with colored water or smear them with colored powders. Afterward, they clean up and celebrate by singing, dancing, and eating sweets made of milk and sugar.

I is for Id al-Noruz, the Persian new year on the first day of spring. Families get together for and they set up a special table with seven lucky pudding, vinegar, garlic, sumac berries, and the Children dress up in new clothes, play with their c and receive gold coins.

K is for k wings, bats, and flies prized kites. but it is also popu children have kite- game is to bring an

L is for the lotus, slowly unfolding its petals. Throughout East Asia, this simple pink-and-white water lily is a symbol of hope and peace. Even in thick and ugly mud, the lotus blossom shoots up pure and unspoiled.

lotus in Hindi

M is for the monsoon, blowing warm, wet winds. Farmers need to finish their planting before the monsoon arrives. Once they're done, they wait anxiously for the badly needed rain. A clap of thunder! Lightning cracks open the sky, and buckets of rain pour down.

مانسون

monsoon in Urdu

H is for Holi, a holiday of chills and thrills. A Hindu festival in India, Holi celebrates the colors of spring. During this holiday, children (and grown-ups) sneak up on their friends and drench them with colored water or smear them with colored powders. Afterward, they clean up and celebrate by singing, dancing, and eating sweets made of milk and sugar.

होली

Holi in Hindi

I is for Id al-Noruz, the Persian new year. Id al-Noruz comes on the first day of spring. Families get together for a large meal of fish, and they set up a special table with seven lucky items: apples, grass, pudding, vinegar, garlic, sumac berries, and the fruit of the lotus tree. Children dress up in new clothes, play with their cousins and friends, and receive gold coins.

نوروز

Id al-Noruz in Persian

J is for jade, stone of heaven. Many people in East Asia wear jade because they believe it will keep them from harm. A beautiful and hard stone, jade comes in a rainbow of pastel colors: yellow, lavender, pink, white, and green. If someone is good and kind, people may call that individual a "jade" person.

ကျောက်စိမ်း:

jade in Burmese

K is for kites, fluttering in the wind. Dragon wings, bats, and butterflies dance in the skies where everyone flies prized kites. Kite-flying is a national pastime in Korea, but it is also popular in other Asian countries. In Malaysia, children have kite-fighting contests where the object of the game is to bring an opponent's kite down to the ground.

연

kites in Korean

P is for the panda, playing peekaboo with a bamboo
shoot. The panda eats mostly bamboo, which it holds with its front paws,
crunching the hard stems with its strong jaw. Once in a while, the panda
will climb a tree to get its favorite snack—honey.

熊猫

panda in Chinese

Q is for the Qur'an, the Muslim holy book. All over the Muslim world, both children and adults compete in singing the poetry of the Qur'an. Singing praises to Allah, a child's voice, pure and clear, rises to heaven.

ٱلقُرآن ٱلكَريم

Qur'an in Arabic

R is for rice, fried, steamed, or curried. Cultivated throughout Asia, rice is eaten many ways. Chinese children have rice soup for breakfast, Indian children eat curried rice, and the children of Saudi Arabia scoop rice with their fingers.

饭

rice in Chinese

S is for sled races on rivers of ice. In the extremely cold winters of Siberia, people use reindeer to pull their sleighs and sleds and race them on the frozen rivers. They also rely on the reindeer for food, clothes, and getting from one place to another.

САНИ
sled in
Cyrillic-Russian

T is for Turkish delight, a chewy treat. Enjoyed by children in Turkey and the Middle East, these small coffee-colored cubes are made of sugar, lemon, gelatin, and pistachio nuts.

LOKUM
Turkish delight in
Turkish

U is for umbrellas,

twirling in the umbrella dance. Invented by the Chinese, umbrellas in Asia are often made of coated paper, cotton, or silk. People use their umbrellas to protect themselves from both rain and sun.

雨傘

umbrella in Chinese

V is for villages, where most Asians still live. Although Asia has some of the world's largest cities, like Tokyo, Seoul, and Bombay, most Asians live in farming villages. The villages where people grow up are an important part of who they are. When introducing themselves, people sometimes give the name of their village before they give their own name.

마을
villages in Korean

W is for the water buffalo, an easy ride through the
rice paddies. This large, lumbering ox is perfect for plowing the fields.
It has specially adapted hooves that keep it from sinking in the mud.

Kalabaw

water buffalo in
Tagalog (Philippines)

X is for xiang qi (siang chi), the game of Chinese chess. Originally brought from India, where it is still popular, Chinese chess is a game of strategy for two players. A crowd of onlookers gathers while the players move their elephants, soldiers, and castles on the board.

象棋
―――
xiang qi in
Chinese

Y is for yurts, the tentlike homes of the Mongolians. Called ger (rhymes with hair) in Mongolian, the yurt is a round structure made with animal skins or thick wool felt covering a wood frame. Made in factories, modern yurts are roomy and inexpensive.

ГЭР
―――
yurt in Mongolian

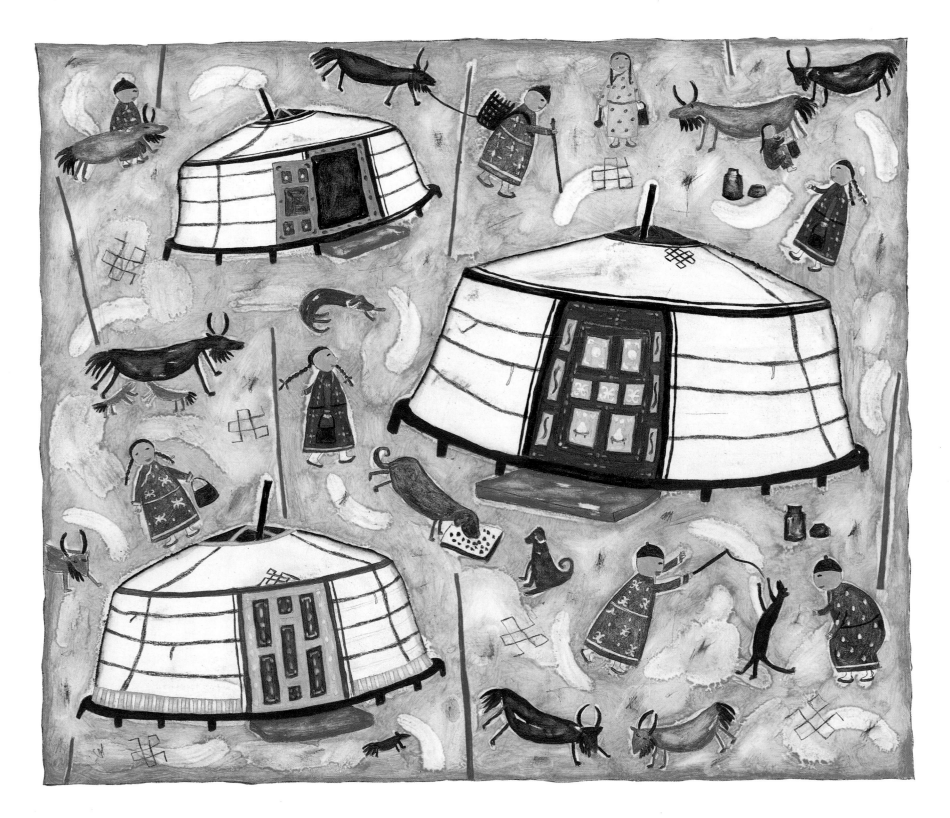

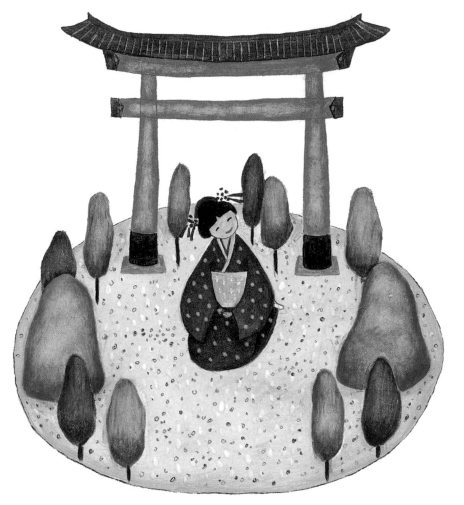

Z is for Zen, which teaches that the world is one. Zen culture, practiced throughout Asia, emphasizes peace and simplicity and a thoughtful, disciplined way of life.

Sitting quietly, doing nothing
Spring comes, and the grass grows by itself.

from the *Zenrin Kushu*

禪
Zen in Japanese